Life on Snow and Ice

Published in the UK by Scholastic Education, 2023
Scholastic Distribution Centre, Bosworth Avenue, Tournament Fields, Warwick, CV34 6UQ
Scholastic Ireland, 89E Lagan Road, Dublin Industrial Estate, Glasnevin, Dublin, D11 HP5F

SCHOLASTIC and associated logos are trademarks and/or registered trademarks of Scholastic Inc.
www.scholastic.co.uk
© 2023 Scholastic
1 2 3 4 5 6 7 8 9   3 4 5 6 7 8 9 0 1 2

Printed by Ashford Colour Press
The book is made of materials from well-managed, FSC®-certified forests and other controlled sources.

A CIP catalogue record for this book is available from the British Library.
ISBN 978-0702-32109-2

All rights reserved. This book is sold subject to the condition that it shall not, by way of trade or otherwise, be lent, hired out or otherwise circulated in any form of binding or cover other than that in which it is published. No part of this publication may be reproduced, stored in a retrieval system, or transmitted in any form or by any other means (electronic, mechanical, photocopying, recording or otherwise) without prior written permission of Scholastic.

Every effort has been made to trace copyright holders for the works reproduced in this publication, and the publishers apologise for any inadvertent omissions.

Author
Ann Hill
Editorial team
Rachel Morgan, Vicki Yates, Abbie Rushton, Jennie Clifford
Design team
Dipa Mistry, Andrea Lewis, We Are Grace
Photographs
Cover (ice) Ukususha/iStock
Cover (penguin) elmvilla/iStock
p4–5 Viacheslav Lopatin/Shutterstock
p6 ginger_polina_bublik/Shutterstock
p7 Nora Yusuf/Shutterstock
p8, 24 vladsilver/Shutterstock
p3, 9 polarman/Shutterstock
p10 Stuedal/Shutterstock
p11 Wirestock/iStock
p12 Fotoyoco/Shutterstock
p13, 24 pixuberant/Shutterstock
p14 ChameleonsEye/Shutterstock
p15 tbarrat/iStock
p16 Peter J. Chesley/Shutterstock
p17 Valerijs Novickis/Shutterstock
p1, 18 rbrown10/Shutterstock
p19, 24 Storimages/Shutterstock
p20 Kerry Hargrove/iStock
p21 Jennifersal/Shutterstock
p22 drferry/iStock
p23 milehightraveler/iStock

Help your child to read!

This book practises these letters and letter sounds.
Point and say the sounds with your child:

- y (as in 'very')
- ea (as in 'weather')
- wh (as in 'when')
- ow (as in 'snow')
- le (as in 'little')
- al (as in 'animal')
- c (as in 'ice')
- ve (as in 'live')
- o–e (as in 'some')
- ou (as in 'young')

Your child may need help to read these common tricky words:

- the
- are
- to
- they
- their
- do
- there
- of
- into
- again

Before reading
- Look at the cover picture and read the title together. Read the back cover blurb to your child.
- Ask your child: *Would you like to live in the Arctic or the Antarctic? Why?*
- Talk about the image in the magnifying glass.

During reading
- If your child gets stuck on a word, remind them to sound it out and then blend the sounds to read the word: s-n-ow, snow.
- If they are still stuck, show them how to read the word.
- Enjoy looking at the pictures together. Pause to talk about the information.

After reading
- Talk about the images on page 24. What can your child tell you about them?
- Ask your child: *Which animals eat plants? What do they do when it gets very cold?*
- Discuss what your child's favourite animal in the book was. What did they like about the animal?

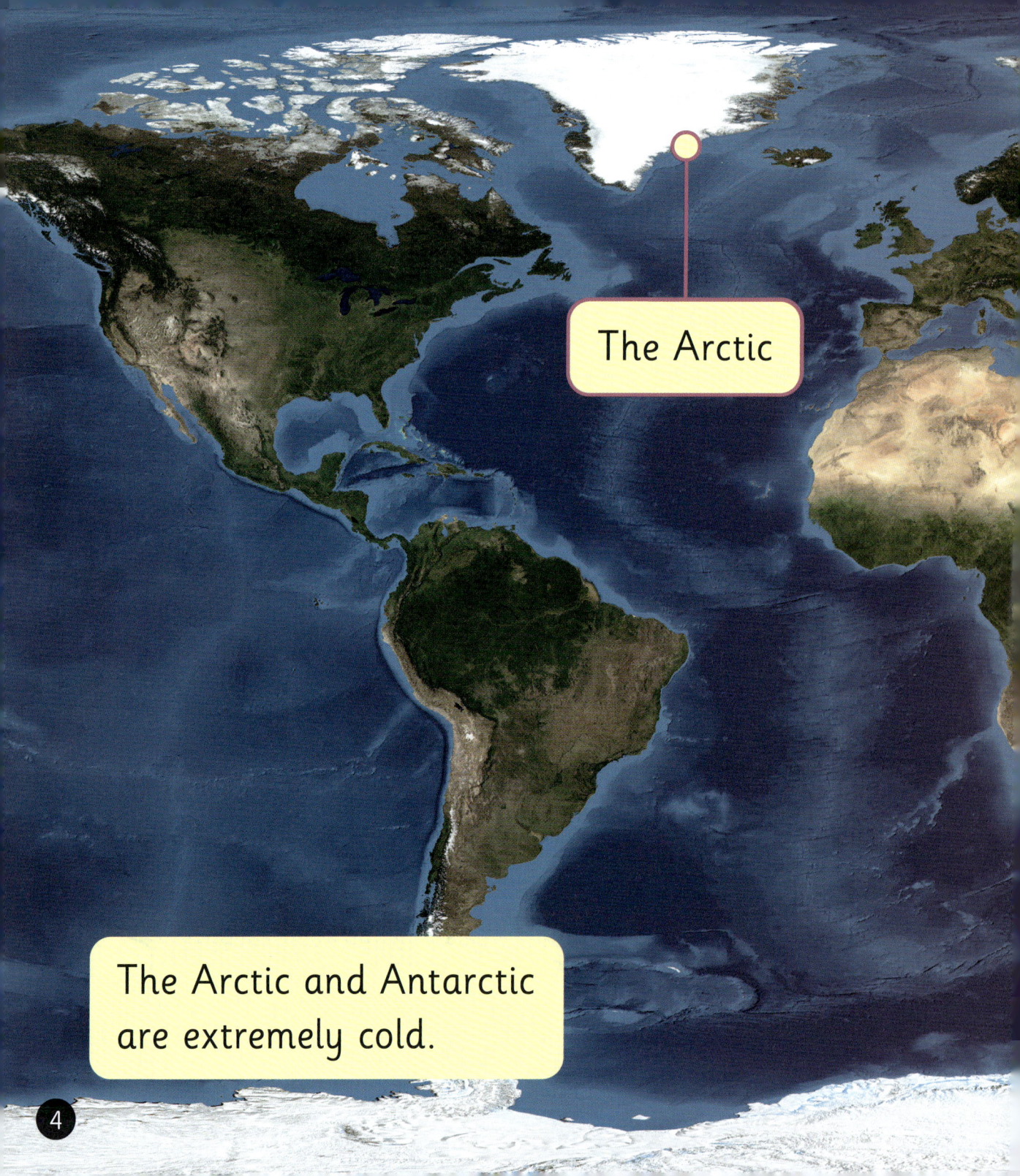

The Arctic

The Arctic and Antarctic are extremely cold.

The Antarctic

It is hard to live in these places.

The Arctic and Antarctic get little sunshine. They have long winters and short summers.

The weather can be very windy. This creates blizzards (snowstorms).

Despite the cold, some animals live in these places with their young.

seabird in a blizzard

How do animals cope with the cold? In the Antarctic, these seabirds huddle up. Dads gently shield young chicks under their soft feathers.

Some gather in massive groups. There can be tens of thousands in total!

Musk oxen nibble on flat Arctic land.

When there is a cold wind, the musk oxen huddle up. Standing shoulder to shoulder keeps them snug.
Younger oxen stay in the middle.

Feathers or thick fur help in ice-cold weather.

Arctic snowy owl

Seals have a layer of fat under their skin. This blubber keeps the chill out.

There is little food on the snow and ice.

Lots of animals find food, like fish, in the sea instead.

When this animal smells a seal under the ice, it grabs it with its claws.

It is not easy to get about on snow and ice. Some animals choose to slide!

flipper

Seals have flippers, so they are good swimmers.

Some animals have big paws so they do not sink into the snow.

Floating ice sheets offer a place to rest between swims.

Lots of animals make dens in the snow.

an Arctic fox in a hollow

Young foxes leave the cosy den when they are around three weeks old.

In summer, the snow melts. The Arctic fox grows a new coat so it can blend into the background.

When the weather is snowy again, the dark hair moults (drops out) and the white hair grows back.

Talk about it!